If THE fUTURE IS A fETISH

YESYES BOOKS ◤ PORTLAND

IF THE

FUTURE

IS A

FETISH

sarah sgro

COVER ART © KATIE TORN, "HALF MOON (POSE 1)," 2017
COVER & INTERIOR DESIGN: ALBAN FISCHER
PROJECT LEAD EDITOR: STEVIE EDWARDS

ISBN 978-1-936919-69-7
PRINTED IN THE UNITED STATES OF AMERICA
LIBRARY OF CONGRESS CATALOGING-IN-PUBLICATION
DATA IS AVAILABLE UPON REQUEST.

PUBLISHED BY YESYES BOOKS
1614 NE ALBERTA ST
PORTLAND, OR 97211
YESYESBOOKS.COM

KMA SULLIVAN, PUBLISHER
STEVIE EDWARDS, SENIOR EDITOR, BOOK DEVELOPMENT
ALBAN FISCHER, GRAPHIC DESIGNER
DEVI GONZALES, MANAGING EDITOR
COLE HILDEBRAND, SENIOR EDITOR OF OPERATIONS
LUTHER HUGHES, ASSISTANT EDITOR & YYB TWITTER
AMBER RAMBHAROSE, EDITOR, ART LIFE & INSTAGRAM
CARLY SCHWEPPE, ASSISTANT EDITOR, *VINYL*
ALEXIS SMITHERS, ASSISTANT EDITOR, *VINYL* & YYB FACEBOOK
PHILLIP B. WILLIAMS, COEDITOR IN CHIEF, *VINYL*
AMIE ZIMMERMAN, EVENTS COORDINATOR
HARI ZIYAD, ASSISTANT EDITOR, *VINYL*

Apologia: ({})[i]

({}) is used throughout to signal fracture, fragmentation, opening. While its shape recalls a womb, ({}) should not conflate maternity with anatomy. ({}) is the body as expanding & hermetic, shameful & vainglorious, an ornate door enclosed between parentheses. ({}) may be pronounced as the mouth around a yellow moon, as Space, the violence of the skin torn.

CONTENTS

({ })

({ })

({ })

({ })

({ })

({ })

({ })

({ })

IF THE FUTURE IS A FETISH

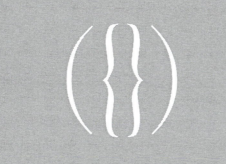

Things I don't allow inside my body: bacon, dildos, anyone who spells my name without an H, major portions of my right hand.

Things I have allowed to stay inside my body: blood, gastric juice, J, A, M, X.

Things I wish to banish from my body: excesses of food, 2mg of Xanax, suicidal thoughts which may not qualify as suicidal thoughts, *nice asssss* texts A when I am streaking drunk, *you have a perfect body* whispers M before I piss onto M's floor, *mmmmmmm* says X at last with my face between the legs of X, *this feels right*, the night I saw a fat & yellow moon, at this point in my life this isn't right, the nights they surface in my dreams, the nights I wake up with my crotch on fire, the nights evolved away from us.

({ })

What is a generative act?

I dream of solitary procreation.

I dream that I am moss expanding into other moss.

I dream of vegetable erotics & I don't mean sticking pickles up my cunt.

To contemplate ecology's   unfathomable intimacies

To imagine pleasures   not genital

My body   stops   starts[ii]

14

I dream   a dark violent revolt [iii]

My body stops   believing in another body

This is how   I reproduce

To insist upon a purity that can't occur. To insist the future is impossible. The death drive me home from school. The death drive in circles round my bed.

When I hold my daughter in my hands. When I menstruate with irregularity & wipe my daughters off my legs. I will name my daughter Red. I will name my daughter Blue. I will name my daughter No. I will name my daughter Yes. I am pregnant with names. J, A, M, X.

I'm waiting in a long line for an ice cream cone I'm at my hometown mall eating samples of the chicken teriyaki sub from Charley's Steakery I'm driving drunk I try to brake I die sorbet the color of my spleen I'm never wearing pants I wake up with my crotch on fire I climax under earthly stress *mmmmmmm* a long line *nnnnnffff* I missed a deadline *guhhhhhhh* there's urine building in some vesicle I squeeze my thighs they slip into my bed I wake up with my crotch on fire I wake before I've had the chance

1. Parent cell.

2. Nucleus divides.

3. Cytoplasm divides.

4. Two new cells (daughter cells).

Do you think it's hot when I bring a blade to my neck.

I want a punk fuck.

I want my best friend in the bathroom while she dyes her hair.

I want a drunk fuck.

Fuck the spilling skin where my jeans split.

Fuck the space I won't fuck.

Fuck the space.

I want a therapeutic fuck.

Anything but 69 we smell each other too much.

I suck your earlobe like a nub of corn.

Fuck me on the ceiling fuck the floor.

Never told you but I want a finger in the butt.

({})

children sing

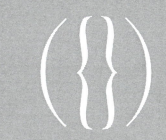

WHEN FALLING (⦃⦄) EMITS A SHARP THUD

Sarah was born a closed system. An extra membrane blanketed her hymen. Tampons would get stuck inside the skin, which unraveled as the long string of a sticky hand she once won from a toy machine. Sarah's mother spread her to extract the saturated cotton. When finally she had it surgically removed the nurses fed her nothing but a pale roll. Sarah avoids large meals. She would like to be small but vicious. Playful but swallows you whole. Sarah is a big whiner. Sarah is a hypersexual. Sarah hears she's queer & silently agrees. Sarah is a dyke. Sarah is a fake. Sarah needs to dig deeper in her work. It's not enough to lift her skirt. Please don't teach her any lessons. In the future she imagines kissing children in a house with cacti she forgets to tend. That is where the future starts & ends. Sarah loves perpetual rebirth. She eats small frequent meals & shits constantly. She hates whatever's sitting in her gut. The (⦃⦄) won't allow itself to be possessed. You cannot suspend the (⦃⦄) in a jar. Sarah would not mind being stretched non-violently. A gentle spreading all her loved ones entering. Sarah was reborn Sarah is an open system Sarah spreads.

A FRIEND CALLS ME MAMA SO I CALL HIM SON

Once again I let myself be eaten
Once again I miss the fat pocket
of my mother's womb no
your stomach's not the womb but here's the snake
like cord whose tip I suck here is where I burrow
feeding like a desperate fawn
I was wrong the problem is my own hunger
Like an infant I will slip
my mouth over everything I touch
Remember how my feet grew first like happy welts
& now they're always in your hands
I'm sick of staring at my face contorting my lips
I've told you how I handle my body in the dark
polishing the weapons
I will use to eat
How I write out ways to touch myself
because I cannot touch myself
beyond the first hungry stroke
I can only ravage so much
white meat from my thighs
before I reach bone
I want to wring my body dry & sell
the blood
I am handing out cookies
on doorsteps I am equipping

those I love with their own exquisite hugs
I want to be everyone's mother
To carry it all in my gut
How many times will I hurl
everyone I know coalescing
like a sudden party in my toilet bowl
Who will squeeze my palm when I am shitting
on a white bed depositing the heads
like a broken ATM
I seal my hole like a faulty spout I bottle
my milk to smell in the dark
crying no they've left me here again
why did they have to come out

ON YOUR BACK PORCH I ATONE

FOR EVERY FUTURE VIOLATION

i don't want to take / you like a taken thing / i address you only in the public sphere / i undress myself alone while dancing / incompletion as a fetish / incompletion as a ripe plum i won't bite / there is talk of space / movement through it / talk of home & multiples / of homes there are your ankles always dangling / from some black upholstered seat / i'm drawn to feet because they're so far / from my hands / for so long i left the warm impression / of my ass in the same plush chair / all i would do was watch *Big Brother* / all i would do was ignore my thighs / those days i was vexed by absence / rather than abundance which is now what vexes me / so many homes so many spaces / i might fill but no one asking me to fill them / i want something demanded of me / hands which shake my body so the breasts ricochet / i am comfortable with bad pipes / i am comfortable with flies congregating round my unflushed shit / matter stilted in its flow / but i am not my excrement / i am a cell in perpetual acceleration / i am a cell imprisoning my thighs / won't somebody demand my thighs / i address you only ever dressed / i address you as motion constantly propelled / riding every tired exhalation as you go / you will run in circles past the chicken tender joint / while i am running in my bed / your toes with small hairs i have watched grow / how in a week from now / as if to say i can / they will grow & grow

BODY AS A PLANT EXPANDING

Everyone's baring fangs that I don't have. These teeth inverted like a yawn inside the womb, breath aerating supple gums. Look how sleek my throat & tongue. Who does not love wet pink skin, fragrant innards of a pork chop, all these fragrant innards that I offer up. Yes I love the violence of flesh the word connoting something gnawed but I no longer want to be a monster. Just today I hated everything with foolish rage & simply jumped in place admiring the symmetry of springing breasts. Listen I have tried my hardest to be gruesome. Consumed the romance of what's decomposed. Clogged my toilet & saved photos of the bowl brimming tall with piss, bundled webs of brown cloth, every piece of me you've never seen. Dreamt about my fingernails decaying dreamt about my stomach dredged in egg wash & filleted. It's hard to be aroused by anything but dirt. Disfiguring my own frame. When I first came in tenth grade my boyfriend laughed like yes I should feel gross shame. All he did was rub his leg against the wishbone of my jeans & I trembled like a baby deer. I closed my eyes & wished to be a spear, something that could pierce. I loved my filth like a weapon. I thought that I could scream instead of come. I feared my skin would not even stick a finger in. Forget about what I have soiled, every dream of being cast in mud. I am donning tiny shorts, slick & luscious like a seal. Sculpting my butt like sculpting my world. Shaving every vagrant hair. It's easier to touch myself when I am soft. My soul like fur my pussy furless. Sometimes when I'm almost there I still feel ill, tiny pulses pulling me apart. I swear I want to bloom. Watch me posing wildly in my bedroom mirror. Singing into every abyss sighing open like a fucking flower. Every pore an orifice & light flooding through. I'm opening I'm opening I'm opening for you.

AUBADE WHICH SWIMS UNTIL IT DROWNS

i wake up tasting pussy or salt & pepper Triscuits, both slick both delight. last night my throat was all slime. my body was a gullet. in the kitchen an intoxicated boy microwaved a slice of pie. i wake up smelling crust i wake up flaking. last night someone told me that i dance like a stream moving down a mountain i cannot be stopped. movement is a violence of its own kind. i slid down each eroded edge i gushed wet. the boy stuck his fork into the pie. i choked up hair. i screamed basement operas. i danced while someone ate my thigh. the boy sticks his face into the pie. i gather what i have shed i gather what i have accrued i walk home asking when the sky will gather light.

WHAT I MEAN IS POEM BUT I'M SLEEPY

no one loves me so i'll write a pome

got home drunk & wrote a pome

smoked a cigarette as an accessory

someone put my pome in a gallery

this pome in minor key

my heart a feral peach

this pome a fuzzy caterpillar

maybe just a worm

at the bar you're sitting

with a handsome man i've never met

in the bathroom

i'm asserting how i'm ugly

lipstick on my teeth

lipstick on my dirt pome

no one texts my pome

back

my pome thirsty

for a hunk of flesh

when i don't eat

i want to kiss whoever

sitting next to me

at least i can come home

to write pome

i love myself

with a fresh hand

i taint my fingers

with tobacco as a fast excuse

to stand

my lips beloooooong

in a pome

my ass beloooooooong

on your lips

i will violate myself

in every pome

& still be safe

no one sleeps beside me

but my words

i will fuck my pome

as you probably expect

i stay sadder

than i ever were

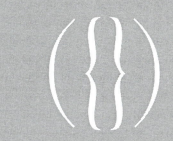

a number of guidelines exist to help / deal with sexuality / increased focus on breasts / pubic hair / teens who will eventually identify as gay, lesbian, bisexual / may turn to the Internet to meet partners / feelings of omnipotence / invincibility / fantasy & masturbation / you did not want to be touched / delayed sexual debut / a history of heterosexual activity / kissed a girl / the implications of transient / activity / have you ever traded / has anyone ever touched / it is not uncommon / although vulnerability / are you / currently spending time with someone special / may "fall in love" / during intercourse / a strong desire / to have an infant is often encountered[iv]

Phenomenology of I'm in hiding

Phenomenology of man at Mississippi bar calls me dyke & I feel seen

Phenomenology of I am trying to dissociate my queerness from my infidelity

Phenomenology of no one cares

Phenomenology of armpit hair

My friends say I look phenomenal

Phenomenology of yes I do

My mother wants to shave me secretly at night but sorry I am a phenomenon

Phenomenology of I have always been a liar

Phenomenology of accountability

I am part of a phenomenon but also I'm alone

Phenomenology of without them I'm immaculate

Phenomenology of I have given birth behind a closet door

Phenomenology of I have given birth without them

To be exited instead of entered is my favorite phenomenon

({})

X: does it feel like there's inertia to the moods

J: like any animal you seek out comfort when you're stressed

J: like any animal you're ugly when in pain

J: i studied crisis management

X: i studied hotel management

A: would you say you are in crisis

M: i prefer

S: when i am sleeping

38 **M:** your pussy shaved

S: i'll prune the leaves with shears

S: i'll lick my membrane smooth

S: i'll suck the moisture from a lake

S: i'm an animal for you

All night I tried to hold J's face. Swaddled a Corona in a tube sock. J inched away. If you could see me now. If you could see me hold the face of M, X, A. My face is an ill-constructed face in that whenever I excuse myself to pee you know I have been weeping. The other day I tried to hold A's hand through a screen. The other day I tried to hold M's gaze. This is all about J A M X my face how much of me you see.

You want to get me off

this couch. I can't

go outside.

My skin thin like an amniotic sac.

My skin the thinning of a cervix when my daughter coming out.

Is there something inherently queer about pregnancy itself, insofar as it profoundly alters one's "normal" state, and occasionally a radical intimacy with—and radical alienation from—one's body? [v]

({})

Sexuality is an issue of orientation, the way our bodies extend into space.
Bodies point to objects. Objects point back.
Objects within reach are not haphazard.
Body-object "coinciding" makes encounter.
To experience a queer phenomenology is to tend towards the unreachable, to transcend bodily "horizons." [vi]
I train my body to become an object.
I rid my life of useless objects.

({})

The future is an issue of orientation, how "now" & "when" coincide.
To experience a queer future is to tend towards the unreachable & survive.

The future relegates familiar objects to the background.

The future transcends bodily horizons.

The future is haphazard.

The future points back.

Hello from the future we have a voice. Hello from your child who is no object. You imagine holding me the way you've hated being held; I must suckle at your tit or I cannot live. It is easy to give into dogma. The other does not always taint the self. Often the self taints the self like this poet & this poem. Often the self taints the child. *Mobius strip.* [vii] You imagine me a clone. You imagine unlike all the others I will stay. I will say I was born with strange myths in my body. I opened my eyes & saw a yellow moon. The word cock flitted in my throat. How could I have known this vulgar word? You will teach me to appreciate every gift that I am given; therefore, I appreciate these myths. I listen but I'll never be a clone. I emerged alone. I emerged with no extra skin. When I left your body it was like I never knew your body. My lungs acclimated quickly to the flood of air. When I sleep I don't imagine I am in a womb. If I do it is a womb from diagrams I've studied, for how could I remember the particular glow of your womb? Perhaps you have imagined that by making me you have built a room. Please do not resent the necessity of doors. My legs swing open like a strange myth in my body.

This is a mother poem ({})

This is a melancholic fucking poem ({})

This poem has no opening ({})

This poem fell & split its womb ({})

It's nobody's responsibility to touch this poem ({})

Often passionate relationships are toxic like this poet & this poem ({})

This poem named her daughter Space ({})

This daughter lives inside this poem ({})

This is a populated room ({})

To remember is to reproduce ({})

I want to have my child & eat her too ({})

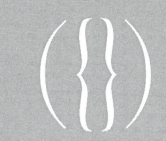

St. Agatha of Sicily is a Christian saint & virgin martyr. After refusing to have sex with a nobleman, Agatha was imprisoned in a brothel & eventually put to death during the persecution of Decius (250–253) for her profession of faith. Amongst the tortures she underwent was the cutting off of her breasts. Agatha is venerated as the patron saint of breast cancer patients, martyrs, wet nurses, bell-founders, bakers, fire, earthquakes, & eruptions of Mount Etna.[viii]

WHEN I ASK WHO IS SPEAKING

I MEAN WHOSE TONGUE

it's a trap   i still mistake the body   beyond reach

for the body of a saint   i have brought a blade   the nipple

swelled   spraying pus against the bathroom wall   i infect you

when i claim your mouth   spread thrush   between the tongues

my tongue was born   in 251 AD   that year the volcano

did not detonate   now i am   alive inside this lush

& land-rich state   without sex   without the body

i have made my saint   if the poem is a living object

if the tongue grows   yeast   & thus it is a living organ   the breast

departed so abruptly   from this poem   this year

i have asked any close volcano   for a small explosion

i am not a martyr   for the things i've taken willingly   inside my throat

UPON INSPECTION OF THESE

SANCTIFYING PORTRAITS

firstly I would like to sever   every metaphor   in which my body is a meal

my breasts are not bread   or anything a man would like to break   & spread

I am no vessel   for the butter in your mouth   I have never salivated

at the legend of my breasts upon a plate   paint my body   & you've made a myth

of all its elements   I am bored by your belief in purity   as supernatural

hunger is an impulse   that I moderate like any other   reason with your hunger

& you realize it is fear or dehydration   the body is equipped   to handle its starvation

I have stored my fat to feed on   which is creamy on its own   which does not need bread

similarly I am satisfied alone   I fall asleep & lose my mind   amid the creamy insides

my thighs emerge   congealed with nectar   from the sun   I was born

with many comforts   instantly a breast inside my mouth   mother-room

which nourished me   yes the supple cord was cleaved   yes I claw the air

when a nipple surfaces in dreams   but I do not desire   what is no longer

affixed to me   if you haven't filled your body adequately   I am not accountable

for all that space   I am not a still life   of your hunger   pressed

against the bed   a sharp thing enters   scalpel in my chest   fork between my legs

If THERE'S A NONMIRACULOUS ANSWER, WE SAY SO

We have carbon dated the Virgin's bones. We have flown to Sicily and back in a cramped aircraft. The countryside is beautiful and if you have the time try the *sfincione* off the street or if you feel adventurous the *pane con la milza* (bread with pork spleen).

$$t = 8267 \cdot \ln (N0 / N) \text{ years} = 19035 \cdot \log (N0 / N) \text{ years}$$

We can only date what was once living. We have used an algorithm. There are stories of the bosoms skewered, molestation, body rolled across a bed of coal.

We took our children hiking at Stromboli. My son said, *Mama can you date a heart?* My daughter said, *Daddy can you date a brain?* Organ meat is an indulgence. We can only date the bones.

$n + 14$

$7N$

$\rightarrow 14$

$6C$

$+ p$

There are legends that the Virgin's veil stopped lava in its tracks. Christ appeared as a hallucination and rebuilt the chest. Miracles are strange events in holy clothing. Carbon-14 decays at a constant rate.

We have measured the residual radiocarbon. We are chemists but we sure deserve a small vacation. We have taken family photographs outside Mt. Etna. It is quiet season now for the volcano so we're safe.

$$^{14}_{6}C \rightarrow\ ^{14}_{7}N + e^- + \nu$$

We have placed the martyrdom in 251 AD. Italy is less congested in the autumn months so we paid lower rates. Miracles are old phenomena. The body senses its impending rupture and evaporates.

CRUEL MAN YOU DARE TO

MUTILATE ME IN THIS WAY

Trauma is a breast for instance:

    The glands branch out like rooms inside a house.

    I run outside without my clothes & the tissue ricochets.

    The house endures the storm but everything inside it breaks.

    I flatten them abidingly I strap the inconvenient weight.

Trauma is non-linear for instance:

    An apparition. When the salve arrives it is St. Peter singing.

    My breast a church inside his mouth.

    I tremble at the thought of being spread.

    I see a stick of butter & I wretch.

    The world returns like a dog to its vomit.

My breasts unleavened discs.

Slice what makes me mother then insist I be your mother saint.

Trauma is historical for instance:

When I am on my knees behind the bathroom door.

That year the volcano did not detonate.

I have made a dry thing wet inside my throat.

I have made an idle object tendrilous.

Do you remember how your mother fed you.

I am running but there is a scalpel in my breast.

I am running I am running & I wretch.

I AM RUNNING I AM RUNNING

a sharp thing enters   & the future has seceded   from my body

martyr of the wet   nurse   martyr for the unborn body

it's november   raw air   whets my tits

i'm erect without intention   for i've scorned   the evening throbs

the sleepless twitch   i wanted the milk   & not the breast

dress my corpse   in layers   for it is november

i have never   met a sharp thing   that has not tried to enter

i wanted a child   born from the moon   from my mouth

S arrives in disarray S arrives sentimental with illusions letters churning in her head this would not ordinarily concern yes we all carry burdens of our negativity the cock that couldn't penetrate a mangled hole taste aversion to an inexpensive spirit such as Sailor Jerry's Silver Rum which scorched the patient's throat provoked the violent disavowal of her bra before her peers who whispered on the architecture of her tits S this would not ordinarily confuse except for your refusal to believe in a redemptive future[ix] demonstrated by a rapid increase in your sleep demonstrated by your nightly intake of Xanax 2mg formerly known as Xanax 1mg S we found the notes beside your bed which read *you could do it & not tell a soul or I want to die & owe nothing to the world except the people I still owe* yes there was the evening everybody left your home you stripped alone you weeped you husk of corn you gripped your phone documenting drunk on video *I feel suicidal when they go* we understand surrender is an easy-sounding quest especially when you are tired especially when everyone has left this is why we are prescribing you a child this is why upon entering this office you were fertilized yes when we mentioned an interest in cleanliness swabbed your body through with sterilizing goo we launched a quiet sperm up into you the details unimportant we are most concerned with treatment S although you dream of death we do not believe that you will kill your child we maintain the sacrament of the unknown its spongy arms body that has not yet gone letter you have not yet chose if we support any construct it's the future understand the scientific drive to last understand *we might survive* is the best we can offer in this circumstance vaginal dryness benzodiazepines / Xanax sleep past noon / suicidal thoughts which may not qualify as suicidal thoughts genetic? / White Plains Hospital reviews / parent-infant theory Winnicott / therapists Connecticut / Xanax anorgasmia / Xanax sleep paralysis / seven forms of non-monogamy / VICE guide to eating pussy like a queen / normal that I want to kill myself but never would? / White Plains Hospital Emergency / aloe vera lube / shea butter lube / benzo use genetic? / how does moss reproduce / hours Luso Taxi / therapists mild depression & anxiety / trauma fear of masturbation / trauma drug abuse / White Plains Hospital Inpatient Services / boundaries open relationship / Kinsey score Buzzfeed quiz / Xanax pregnant dangerous / trauma I don't wanna live / baby names No / baby names Yes / if moisture permits

{{}}
Whatever information women possess of their own bodies.[x]

I hold J's body to my body & there is no revelation. For J's body is no copy of my body. For we are boundaries with disparate anatomies.

{{}}
The clitoral body & the desires of the chaste friend.

I'm depressed so I take Xanax 2mg & you're depressed so you do not want sex. We watch TV because an image moving is a generative act. We watch a plot unfold & then rebuild after the screen goes black. My clit hangs like a grandpa clock. My pussy smooth but for this ample clot.

{{}}

The figure of the tribade is represented as the outgrowth of a monstrous bodily morphology, insofar as she functions more generally as a metaphor for excessive and unruly female desire.

When we are at the party making out against my kitchen wall, I am a jock unfurling my impressive musculature unto J. I have unhitched the bra of J beneath a v-neck blouse in public space. When we are driving home, I don a hat & walk J to J's door. I am a cowboy demonstrating celebrated valor. I drape my cape across J's shoulders.

J says *that's some gay shit* & that's right. Behold the macroclitoride! The tommie! Female husband to my lady bride! My clit balloons. My clit grows like a mushroom patch, baby clits germinating on my thighs.

{{}}
What it means to be a lesbian, of course, depends on what it means to make love.

You are tiny waiting to be found: classical pursuit of pearl inside its shell. This doesn't mean you're delicate; it's just the way you're made. I slide a finger back & forth inside you as to penetrate. My clit an oaf who cannot hide. The shame of rubbing is you cannot give me what I want until I beg.

the mosses aren't helpless / to make a home for water / they become bisexual / mosses were made for the boundary layer / species have evolved / without gender / without a male in sight / *D. scoparium* / *D. polysetum* / *D. flagellare* / the right mate / passes over the surface like a rock / a warm, moist habitat / interacts in interesting ways with what it touches / heaven knows there are plenty of us / suspended in drought-sleep / a dry moss is incapable of growth / the good news is that there will be offspring / *D. montaum* / *D. fulvum* / *D. undulatum* / heaven knows there are plenty of us already [xi]

This isn't a love poem to the trees

The trees were never sacred

My shit is just as sacred as the trees

for it makes & then sustains the trees

My desires have always been the same

to inhabit other bodies

I am permeable for I am capable

of rendering a child bloody

in your nervous hands

Every body is assaulted

the trees by wind & rain

myself by wind & rain

I love to eat so many salted nuts at night

that my stomach swells like I am pregnant

I love this human body for what it contains

I love to shit for its terminal release

The exodus of one thing grows a blossom

like a rose stem or a bloody head

My ecology is all consuming

My revolt is unforgiving

My body a delicious boundary

S: if you're up can we talk

J: about last night sorry but i don't think we should test that door again

X: vchat in 10?

X: heating up mac n cheese

X: wish you were eating with me

J: ever since we broke up i'm so horny

S: when we talk i want to die

A: do you ever think about how

S: i want to die

A: we want to get the most pleasure out of life in the most convenient way

S: woooooow deep

M: how you be these days?

S: sorrrry kind of drunk but just admit whenever we're together we have crazy chemistry

A: do you remember eating meat

S: i think it's ok to be tender

1.

I bring a blade to my neck   I dream of sucking on the ear of X   in reconciliation

whispering *you missed me*   or you tried to take me   with the skin intact   or I offered

myself up unharmed   I brought chocolate pudding to my bed   prepared my body

to be licked & spread   X tried to take me   or I begged   his X would never

fit for the skin was indestructible   filled   with cotton which my mother would extract

X left   me with the skin intact   tangled up around her thumb   my mother

would detangle me   this woman ache   I am allowed to keep   the cotton plug

emerged unclean   we screamed   we mourned my child   the space

that X did not create   for he does not return   I am displaced   nothing

has been born   for like the moon   for like my skin   when it has torn

2.

A puts me in my place   swathes my butt in scented cream   still I leave   my blood

across his sheets   the puddle wet   the other woman wet   across his sheets

an hour after I have left   I smell   my children   on her thighs

I'm warning you   release my almost-child   yes she died

but she is mine   like something died   with A   but it's still mine

like I have seen the face   of J encroach   in doggy-style   my other woman

is a moat   around my cunt   A's other woman   wears my menstrual coat

A will never   put me in my place   he loves me so he stays   I stay   69

3.

M I'm sorry   you are indistinct   a pocket knife   housed in True Religion jeans

you called them titties   took me mangled   I woke up with my mouth inside your jeans

I woke up pissing on your floor   I scrubbed the stain on both knees   my mouth

a fat moon   I don't have much to say   I've already given you my mouth

where was ({})   of my latent dreams   please leave   I am a cavern

only for myself   my thirsty child   needs a room   inside of me

4.

With J I'm not responsible   for moisture   everything we need   J supplies

if you give a mouth a pussy   no one's dry   at this point in your life   this

isn't right   I write a lousy poem   out of spite   the night we see a yellow moon

I write an awful note & hide   the note inside my drawer   I swallow Xanax 2mg

I message A expressing love   I message J expressing thirst   I don't remember

who I heard from first   congratulations I am queer   blessings I can stretch

an orifice to see what fits   all the meat is sour   all my tongues are tendrilous

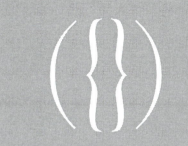

YUM

my rapture

mmmm a Heath Bar shake from Baskin Robbins

is the most

caloric beverage in America

according to *Eat This, Not That*

eat this: my pussy

on a good day

is still arid

edible matter

the most wholesome things

are not always the most toothsome

there is no such thing as an animal

not transformed

by all of its encounters

find me a body

still intact

YUM Kristeva

mmmm my mother

everyday i eat my unborn child

as a light snack

I EMERGED WITH HIS

NORTH FACE ADORNING MY BREASTS

eight shots in i fuck the gleaning   titan of my hometown in a bathroom   tits angry stones
& i have wanted this so long   the irony of other muscles   pressing on my mangled bones
knuckles that have punched a man   prying me   apart   i spread open

the door & throw my bra across the basement   as a party favor, guests ogling   the leopard
cups   go ahead: lick the crevices   looking for my milk   i'm the animal
that never comes, dried-out pussy hanging   on the shower door   in dreams

my thighs go wet at images   of men who'd never fuck me   (but now in this dream
they're fucking me)   i wake exploding   heavy   bladder pressing on my crotch
how it happened in the bathroom: he tells me i have nipples   like a porn star & i moan

as though this is our movie set   unfurling   as a bath mat on the floor   of course it can be fun
to be the object   of desire of control your fingers   which deposit dirt into my tidy hole
i've spent whole evenings propping up my breasts   wishing to be filled   i used to have

nothing to my name   no broth beneath this skin but tepid blood   before bed i reached
into my throat for any sort of coin   tried pulling bodies from my gut   could i dream myself
to being whole & then embalmed   who would i have to tell   what would i have   to touch

77

I OWN MY SEXUALITY

you asked for it
i like blunt pressure
dick i like shallow
can't be mine
on my own
i'll swallow it whole
i'm a cavern
hearing 'bout
shall i find another
shaped want
the diamond in my mouth
my smell
through flared jeans
has no doors
when i thrust a finger in
i will rub against exterior
of an empty bed
if this is a porno i am fording
in the smallest boat
i'd like to leave the world

i don't care if you never did
give me foot thigh tumescent
wet licks boys girls whatever
i do believe i'm most buoyant
if you buy me a dildo
sorry
are you sick of
my poor sweet cunt
lexicon for my claw
parched weed bald debris
i can't say i remember
except when i am bleeding
the strongest exit
i feel nothing
give me the hearty gourd
planets give me the edge
if this is floating i am never full
a grotto
i'd like to lick some tits
through a fragrant hole

THIS ROAD IS NO BRIGHTER THAN THE LAST FEW

I drive home so fast I drive home effacing every object in my path. Gray pedestrians. Raccoons that haven't even left the womb. I forget to signal left I forget about the man topless on a futon waiting for my call. Once he stuck his foot into my mouth & dragged his toes across my gums until I coughed up laughs like blood. We made love. Every other month he asks me delicately why I never come. I say I'm comfortable dispensing gifts like chips sliding down the gutter of a trustworthy machine. I don't crave the salt the oil congealing at the bottom of my gut. Once he brought a plastic cock ring from the CVS into our bed. I pressed a button & it quivered unabashedly around his shaft he entered me the sound like a doll who dances when you pull its string I laughed I laughed. This home has no sound. Before bed I ask myself if I am being eaten who should be the tongue. How starving I am to be loved & forget that love. How late I am for some event I cannot drive any faster than I am. Move aside fledgling raccoon! Watch out tender man! I dig my foot into the gas I dig my foot into my mouth. I roll my window down & a moth enters through the crack.

I WEAR MY MAN OUT

on the town like a coat / i curl up in his cured hide / i hear *pelts* & think of shit not skin / confusing it for *pellets* / my man is more shit than skin / he defecates often he is so thin / i wear my man's shit / in between my legs / you think this is vile / you think i am obsessed / with smearing shit up & down my legs / i'm just saying i desire any coat / he can give / have you noticed how we shrink / in tandem occupying a collective void / i mean honey / i shrunk my lover it is dire / i mean my man performs / two hundred fifty push-ups / after swallowing an ice cream cone / before fucking we apologize / for gaining weight & fucking other women / in our different homes / we occupy a collective toilet bowl / our fuck develops peach fuzz / i won't pretend to be a wolf / for the sake of this poem / i refuse to nourish / anyone in this poem / this poem is an expulsion / pulling you / around my waist gagging / at how sweet how cold

[MY BODY DIES THE MORE I USE IT]

my body dies the more I use it
so I use it often / there a tender

death wish / terrifying entrance /
when I panic it's from choking

on three separate tongues / mine
my lover's & a tired history

of loss / what I use my body for
today is running & a mediocre poem

which I use for therapy / it works
temporarily / any small re-entrance

is a sign of progress / writing down
the trauma for the first time is still

trauma / writing down the trauma
for the fifth time is still trauma but

at least I have a poem in my hands /
my lover is resilient / peeling back

a sleeve she shows me ghost incisions /
slice your skin & you're no longer

in a poem or a metaphor / you are
here with a paperclip inside your wrist /

does the past decay the more I use it
in a poem / can I out-poem the past

from churning in my belly-pit / yes
the future is an enzyme & a catalyst

or a burp that smells like hotdogs
& a little like my grief / I hate that

stupid constant place which refuses
tense / longing too / greedily I suck

my lover's upper lip looking for a poem
or I lick the balmy archive of my gut

with all three tongues / one says *loss*
one says *loss* one says *I am not your tongue*

ELEGY FOR MY BUSH & OTHER LUSHNESS

i love being thin enough to slice   of course you die   from the pocket knife   slender

bloodline trailing towards the floor   my right-now lover is a horse   decaying in the center

of the road   who runs over a horse   who sucks the entrails from his butt   leaving him

a tender husk   we fall asleep carved-out   we eat food   that turns our feces green

we are very regular   i carve him out of every private dream   i kiss a girl he doesn't know

i wake adorned   in piss & can't remember   who i love   all my former fucks refuse

to be decrepit   they shed their hair inventively   they buy silver shoes with no strings

in bed i map out   ways to modify my body   i'll wear my bowels as a scarf   i'll wax

the backwoods of my crotch   into a strip   dewy steak   to dig your teeth into   83

here is where the aesthetician skins   my cunt with tiny licks   here is where my lover licks

the puckered skin around my cunt   a little too far to the right   though i don't touch myself

enough to be a guide   if you could please ravage this succulent valley   if you could please

suck this ravishing valley   i value my rapture the curdled scum   the ({ })

does not supply a fill   the ({ }) a bucket in the sand   granules delicious wet

my lover swells   inside me   like a cheeseburger digesting painfully   i vomit

up the shape of a girl   he doesn't know   how she tastes   in a dark room

i am not the void   i own nothing of the void   i own nothing i have   vomited it up

here our dwindled bodies   here my skin recoiling   here my puss a neat frontier

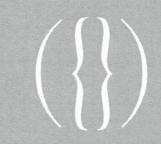

({}) ({}) ({}) ({}) ({}) i love a new day
realizing an excellent idea ({}) ({}) ({})
({}) ({}) ({}) ({}) ({}) ({}) is now just okay
all hail the advent of a door ({}) ({}) ({})
({}) ({}) ({})({}) all praise the future tense
without them ({}) ({}) ({}) ({}) ({}) ({})
({}) ({}) ({}) ({}) ({}) ({}) ({}) i survive
i'm filled with gratitude ({}) ({}) ({}) ({})
({}) ({}) ({}) ({}) ({}) enough to titty fuck
the sky ({}) ({}) ({}) ({}) ({}) ({}) ({})
({}) ({}) ({}) ({}) ({}) ({}) without them
i run from no one ({}) ({}) ({}) ({}) ({})
({}) ({}) ({}) ({}) ({}) ({}) ({}) or i run
for president ({}) ({}) ({}) ({}) ({}) ({})
({}) ({}) ({}) ({}) ({}) ({}) ({}) of my life
that one was corny ({}) ({}) ({}) ({}) ({})
({}) ({}) ({}) ({}) ({}) have you noticed
a motif of corn ({}) ({}) ({}) ({}) ({}) ({})
({}) ({}) ({}) ({}) throughout this poem
it wasn't on purpose ({}) ({}) ({}) ({}) ({})
({}) ({}) ({}) ({}) ({}) ({}) ({}) ({}) at first
i like an unintended thing ({}) ({}) ({}) ({})
({}) ({}) ({}) ({}) ({}) to move me forward

growth requires

one body

i'm a plant & thus

a stunning alternative

to decay [xii]

S: you there it's been 10 min

S: i lick the absence from my paws

S: i grow the absence like a garden on my skin

the jugular   is a substantial vein   I bring   I bring a blade

I bring   death   is not a public space   death is no one's

private joke   I will not condone you celebrating   any decomposing body

or the recreation   of a body like my own   when I wake up

from a dream & finally I'm queer   when I'm never going back   to sleep

I will not romanticize the hollow   of my throat   licked

by Xanax 2mg like marrow from a bone   the jugular engorged   with blood the testicles engorged   my memory   rejects   your sperm

my jugular rejects   the blade   I pledge allegiance   to tumescence

make my life   a public space   look   my recreation

a parade   I hoist my lovers like balloons   reject the possibility   of weight

Watching *Bring It On* throbs searing through my pants. Watching music videos by 50 Cent while giving J bad head. I come before the first scene of a Stanley Kubrick film. I come inside my True Religion jeans. Because a history of thirst you think I'm always wet. My dry is radically uncompromised my aridness an all-pervasive child. My ({}) should be not be understood as innocence although it's obvious I crave protection. J did not want sex & thus he did protect my cunt from rupturing. I ruptured surgically the skin removed with sterile shears. To embrace the possibility of future. To refuse to reproduce their faces yes the letters I have named & too the surgeon's mask & too the fat & yellow moon which promised no one. Here the queer positioned in a room with black-out shades. Here the queer positioned with her thumb inside her throat. I am the narcissistic all-pervasive child staying antisocial helps me stay self-actualized. Will death return the things they take. My pussy skin they take with gloves. J laughs loud when he takes my pioneering cum. I take 2mg of Xanax every day I take the tremors & the wet. Every day I mother things a poem or a turd but I want my daughter too. This desire I accede to. This my sunniest jouissance. My daughter never negativity or irony. My daughter never any other face. With daughter I am never death & though they slip into my bed they will never make me death. I force them out. I cradle what they take & wrap it in a quilt. I kiss the wet jouissance on her new mouth. I kiss the possibility of future.[xiii] Without them. Without them I am still.

If the future is a fetish. If my pussy is a sick fixation. If my pussy can't be fixed. For like the field it has no doors. For like a business it has several partners. For like the future I'm a port. If the future dreams of ({ }). If the future is a tentacle emerging from my body. If the future is an ocean floor. For X is a tentacle pulsing. For J is a tentacle pulsing. If I reproduce as a compulsion. There is me & there is me & there is me & when my child finally arrives with organs pulsing. If I have my child then tape up every hole. If my memory is a stranger. If they never leave me for they do not enter. There is me & there is me & I will reassemble. If not all departures are abandonments. If my child is healthy she will grow. If I am generous & recognize you thirst for things I cannot know. I will reassemble. I am branded by no letters. If they leave. I let them.

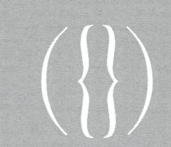

ACKNOWLEDGMENTS

Poems in this manuscript have previously appeared in the following publications; endless gratitude to their editors:

ANMLY: "Upon Inspection of These Sanctifying Portraits"

The Boiler: "[Whatever information women possess]"

Cloud Rodeo: "[Hello from the future]"

DREGINALD: "[S: if you're up]," "[S arrives in disarray]," "[Phenomenology of]," " When Falling Her Cunt Emits A Sharp Thud"

Deluge: "On Your Back Porch I Atone For Every Future Violation," "A Friend Calls Me Mama So I Call Him Son," "Aubade Which Swims Until It Drowns"

glitterMOB: "Body as a Plant Expanding"

Horse Less Review: "This Road Is No Brighter Than The Last Few"

The Offing: "I Own My Sexuality"

Muzzle: "I Wear My Man Out"

Reality Beach: "[my body dies the more I use it]"

Tagvverk: "[If the future is a fetish]," "[The jugular is a substantial vein]," "Elegy for My Bush & Other Lushness," "YUM," "What I Mean Is Poem But I'm Sleepy"

TYPO: "I Emerged With His North Face Adorning My Breasts"

Portions of this manuscript were published as a chapbook called "Without Them I Am Still A Mother" (Letter [r] Press 2017).

———

Immense gratitude to the YesYes Books team for seeing this book and imagining its future. Thank you especially to KMA Sullivan and Stevie Edwards for their thoughtful edits and guidance.

I'm forever filled with love and appreciation for the brilliant faculty at the University of Mississippi MFA program. Thank you for caring about me as a writer and a person and for fueling my craft with warmth and rigor. I am especially grateful to my wonderful thesis committee members Derrick Harriell, Beth Ann Fennelly, and Ari Friedlander for their generous feedback and friendship.

Impossible love to all my ethereal Oxford writer pals: Maggie Woodward, Kina Viola, Marty Cain, Jeffrey Lance, Andrew Dally, Jan Verberkmoes, Alison Levin-Rector, Doug Mitchell, Finn Udall, Julian Randall, Amy Lam, Nadia Alexis, Helene Achanzar, Tyriek White, Lara Avery, Eric Delp, Reggie Fontenot, and so many more. Thank you to everyone who has seen drafts of these poems and contributed your time to their growth.

Sage, Jeff, Amanda: you are my forever friends and sources of support. Cuz, Sana, Julie, Kenny, Deb: I'm so lucky you're my family. Thank you for loving me and roasting me with equal fervor.

Sid and Stink, I love you and I'm so glad you're my huckleberries.

Mom, you have endlessly supported me and my work with your whole heart. We've experienced—will always be experiencing—the worst possible thing. You are my eternal bestie, and together we're surviving.

Dad, I miss you every day. I wish more than anything that I could celebrate with you. Every day I am celebrating with you.

NOTES

[i] My apologia on ({ }) is indebted to Gabrielle Calvocoressi's "Note to the Reader" at the start of her collection *Rocket Fantastic*.

[ii] Collaged language from Marjorie Swann's essay "Vegetable Love: Botany and Sexuality in Early Modern England."

[iii] The phrase "a dark violent revolt" is excerpted from Julia Kristeva's essay "Powers of Horror: An Essay on Abjection."

[iv] Collaged language from Trisha Tulloch's and Miriam Kaufman's article on "Adolescent Sexuality" from *Pediatrics in Review* (January 2013).

[v] From Maggie Nelson's book *The Argonauts*.

[vi] Sara Ahmed posits these ideas in her book *Queer Phenomenology*.

[vii] The image of a "mobius strip" is used to describe a phenomenon of reciprocity in Maggie Nelson's book *The Argonauts*.

[viii] History compiled from "Agatha of Sicily" (Wikipedia).

[ix] Italicized language from Valerie Traub's book *The Renaissance of Lesbianism in Early Modern England*.

[x] Collaged language from Robin Wall Kimmerer's book *Gathering Moss: A Natural and Cultural History of Mosses.*

[xi] From Shannon Kelley's critical essay "The King's Coral Body: A Natural History of Coral and the Post-Tragic Ecology of *The Tempest.*"

[xii] Italicized phrases are excerpted from Lee Edelman's book *No Future.*

PHOTO BY BROOKE BASTIE

SARAH SGRO is the author of the full-length collection *If The Future Is A Fetish* (YesYes Books 2019) and the chapbook *Without Them I Am Still A Mother* (Letter [r] Press 2017). Sgro earned her MFA in Poetry from the University of Mississippi and is pursuing her Ph.D. in English at SUNY Buffalo, where she studies waste in relation to gender and futurity. She previously served as Poetry Editor for the *Yalobusha Review* and as an editorial assistant for *Guernica*, and she currently reads poetry submissions for *Muzzle*. Her work appears in *BOAAT, Anomaly, Cosmonauts Avenue, DREGINALD, The Offing*, and other journals.

ALSO FROM YESYES BOOKS

Full-Length Collections

Ugly Music by Diannely Antigua

i be, but i ain't by Aziza Barnes

The Feeder by Jennifer Jackson Berry

Gutter by Lauren Brazeal

What Runs Over by Kayleb Rae Candrilli

This, Sisyphus by Brandon Courtney

Love the Stranger by Jay Deshpande

Blues Triumphant by Jonterri Gadson

Ceremony of Sand by Rodney Gomez

Undoll by Tanya Grae

North of Order by Nicholas Gulig

Everything Breaking / For Good by Matt Hart

Meet Me Here at Dawn by Sophie Klahr

I Don't Mind If You're Feeling Alone by Thomas Patrick Levy

Sons of Achilles by Nabila Lovelace

Reaper's Milonga by Lucian Mattison

If I Should Say I Have Hope by Lynn Melnick

Landscape with Sex and Violence by Lynn Melnick

GOOD MORNING AMERICA I AM HUNGRY AND ON FIRE by jamie mortara

some planet by jamie mortara

Boyishly by Tanya Olson

Stay by Tanya Olson

a falling knife has no handle by Emily O'Neill

Pelican by Emily O'Neill

The Youngest Butcher in Illinois by Robert Ostrom

A New Language for Falling Out of Love by Meghan Privitello

I'm So Fine: A List of Famous Men & What I Had On by Khadijah Queen

American Barricade by Danniel Schoonebeek

The Anatomist by Taryn Schwilling

Gilt by Raena Shirali

Panic Attack, USA by Nate Slawson

[insert] boy by Danez Smith

Man vs Sky by Corey Zeller

The Bones of Us by J. Bradley
  [Art by Adam Scott Mazer]

Chapbook Collections

Vinyl 45s

  After by Fatimah Asghar

  Inside My Electric City by Caylin Capra-Thomas

  Dream with a Glass Chamber by Aricka Foreman

  Exit Pastoral by Aidan Forster

  Pepper Girl by Jonterri Gadson

  Of Darkness and Tumbling by Mónica Gomery

  Bad Star by Rebecca Hazelton

  Makeshift Cathedral by Peter LaBerge

  Still, the Shore by Keith Leonard

  Please Don't Leave Me Scarlett Johansson by Thomas Patrick Levy

  Juned by Jenn Marie Nunes

  A History of Flamboyance by Justin Phillip Reed

  Unmonstrous by John Allen Taylor

  Giantess by Emily Vizzo

  No by Ocean Vuong

  This American Ghost by Michael Wasson

Blue Note Editions

Beastgirl & Other Origin Myths by Elizabeth Acevedo

Kissing Caskets by Mahogany L. Browne

One Above One Below: Positions & Lamentations by Gala Mukomolova

Companion Series

Inadequate Grave by Brandon Courtney

The Rest of the Body by Jay Deshpande